MW01039047

All Men are **ASSHOLES**

All Women are **BITCHES**

A Humorous Look at the Differences Between Men and Women

JUDIE JEWEL
With
Dan Dourson and Jacob Marlin
Illustrated by J. P. Sulliver
2015

Copyright © 2015 Judie Jewel, Dan Dourson, and Jacob Marlin
Cartoons ©2015 by JP Sulliver

All rights reserved.
Reproduction of any section including cartoons is prohibited without written permission from the authors or cartoonist.

Goatslug Publications
Stanton, KY 40380
Email: judiejewel@gmail.com
Website: www.judiejewel.com

ISBN#: 978-0-692-41903-8

Available on Amazon.com

Follow us on Facebook, Twitter and Instagram @allmenareassholes

Cover Design by: JP Sulliver and Dan Dourson

Disclaimer:

The ideas put forth in this book do not promote, condone, or excuse ANY behavior that is violent or morally, and socially unacceptable including enslavement, objectification, mutilation, or psychological abuse of any kind. Furthermore these views are not necessarily shared by Goatslug Publications or the cartoonist but are solely the views of the authors.

Contents

All Men Are Assholes

Preface

"Everybody's an asshole." ~ Anonymous

This off-the-cuff quote made by a friend years ago was the catalyst for many lively discussions throughout the years, eventually morphing into the title *All Men Are Assholes, All Women Are Bitches.*

My male collaborators and I are not psychologists, psychiatrists, or anthropologists. I am an educator, and they are biologists. Our credentials come from of the school of hard knocks, with a total of six marriages between us, and a willingness to be open-minded, honest, and to laugh at ourselves as well as others. We present provocative, alternative perspectives to the age-old conflict between the sexes—but we do not pretend to have all the answers. If you want *real* relationship help, you probably need to look elsewhere.

Between your gasps, head-shaking, and shrieks of incredulity, we hope you come away with a different perspective in the battle between the sexes, and have a few laughs along the way!

~Judie, Dan, and Jacob

> **WARNING! If just the title of this book makes you cringe, the carrot up your ass is way too deep; pull it out a bit, relax, and enjoy the book, or put it down and walk away—the choice is yours.**

Acknowledgements

Many thanks to JP Sulliver, who adeptly turned our concepts into hilarious and thought-provoking cartoons. Your skillful interpretation and art greatly enhanced the book.

We appreciate the love, support, and encouragement (often amid raised eyebrows) from our family and friends. Time spent brainstorming ideas and laughing uncontrollably was such fun! Thanks, also, to Pattie Batchman for stimulating conversation directing us to research the origins of some of our most widely held beliefs.

A word of gratitude to Dr. Helen Fisher for her extensive research and insights into the biological origins of human behavior, especially human sexual behavior. Interestingly, the book was well underway when a colleague suggested her works as a reference. Much to our delight, her research supported some of our theories. For a complete list of her groundbreaking, entertaining work, check out the references in the back.

Finally, a very special thanks to our good friend and fellow author, Sondra Allan Carr, for her advice, information, and enthusiasm. Her willingness to share her experiences, both positive and negative, was invaluable.

**Dedicated to
assholes and bitches everywhere
Thanks for the inspiration!**

1

All Men Are...All Women Are...

If history has taught us anything, it is that passion and desire are not the same as truth. ~E. O. Wilson

Countless words, boundless volumes, songs, art, and dance have been dedicated to the pursuit of harmonious coexistence between the sexes. The stark differences between males and females call for honesty and a bit of humor if we are to bridge the vast expanses that divide us. After all, Women are from Mars and men are from Penis (oops, I meant, Venus). Or something like that.

Attempts to *delicately* explain and excuse our inescapable disparities have often avoided some cold, *hard* facts. Take a look at the *bulging* stacks of divorce decrees that fill our courtrooms and shelves of self-help books on the subject. Clearly this approach is not working!

It's time to throw civility out the window and get down in the mud and muck to expose our collective soft underbellies.

The truth may be *hard to swallow* but let's face it—**ALL MEN ARE ASSHOLES AND ALL WOMEN ARE BITCHES!**

This bold statement applies to any couple, regardless of sexual preference. Whether you are heterosexual, lesbian, gay, bi-sexual or transsexual (LGBT), in any relationship, there is always one ASSHOLE and one BITCH!

It is not easy to admit we are anything but walking saints, yet if we are honest, *everyone* has acted like an asshole or a bitch at some point in time—yes, even YOU. Maybe no one dared to call you that to your face, but you can bet it was uttered under someone's breath or behind your back! If you don't believe your sainted mother or dad could EVER act that way, just go ask your parents!

Having a hard time thinking about your beloved in these terms? Just remember the levels can vary widely—from the ultimate to the unintentional asshole or bitch—and everything in between!

Is there an explanation for our bad behavior? Biology and evolution provide some of the ingredients. Mix in a shitload of convoluted social and moral constraints that contradict our basic biology, and you have the perfect recipe for assholes and bitches.

Whether this book finds a prominent place on your bedside table for quick access, in the reading room (aka bathroom) where you can ponder its contents or it ends up as a substitute for toilet paper on your next camping trip, we hope it at least provokes thought. In the midst of your gasps or guffaws, maybe you will come a little closer to understanding and getting along with your potential, current, or future asshole or bitch.

What Do You *Mean*?

What do you mean when you call someone an asshole or bitch? Maybe it's the lowest of the low—someone you just can't stand to be around at any time. *My boyfriend slept with my best friend! What an asshole!* Or maybe you're just frustrated with someone's actions. *Stop being such an asshole and listen to me!* The words might be used as a term of endearment to playfully tease—*You just won the lottery? You bitch!* It all depends on the circumstances. Here are some commonly held definitions. If they don't work for you, add your own!

Asshole

1. Any male species (including *Homo sapiens*)
2. A body part used for the removal of waste.
3. A guy who has sex or tries to have sex with every woman he meets (including your sister or best friend).
4. An egotistical male on a power trip who could care less who he steps on to get what he wants.
5. A guy who knocks up your daughter then ditches her.
6. An insensitive prick.
7. Write your own definition here. _____
   _____
   _____

Bitch

1. Any female species (including *Homo sapiens*)
2. A female dog. (*slang*)
3. A woman who will have sex with everyone but you.
4. A drama queen that makes everyone's lives around her miserable.
5. A control freak who thinks she's always right; constantly corrects everyone.
6. An annoying whining female who is not happy with anything their asshole does or says.
7. Write your own definition here._____
   _____
   _____

Life is All About ASS

You're either *married* to an ASS.

Divorced from an ASS or *trying to forget* an ASS.

You're either *working, sweating*

or

laughing your ASS off,

You're *kicking* ASS or *kissing* ASS,

Spanking ASS, *hauling* ASS, *wiping* ASS, *busting* ASS

Trying to get a piece of ASS, OR you *are* an ASS.

~Author Unknown~

2

A Matter of Perspective

I have not failed. I have just found 10,000 ways that won't work. ~Thomas Edison

So how did a middle-aged woman of the Baby Boomer generation who grew up in the Bible Belt write a book with such a provocative title and controversial ideas? It began nearly twenty years ago, when I met my current spouse. Notice I said *current*. I was fresh off of divorce number two—yes two!—trying desperately to understand what went wrong. If there was a chance for me to muster the courage to go down the relationship road again, it would require a radical change in thinking, and a better understanding of the opposite sex. Is this even possible?

I don't know about most women, but as a teen I didn't have a clue about how the male mind worked—or didn't work! I expected guys to act and think like females—emotionally and with sensitivity. Steamy romance novels of my pre-teen years only intensified my warped perspective, setting the stage for further disappointment. With these unrealistic expectations, I entered the wonderful world of dating and began the search for the perfect man, my soul mate. I would have had a better chance of finding a unicorn!

Two marriages and two divorces later, I was no closer to comprehending males than when I was a teen. The LAST thing on my mind after the second failed marriage was another relationship. I was convinced all men WERE assholes! Then I met my current husband, who is undoubtedly the most direct, blunt, and honest person I have ever known.

I know what you are thinking. Who in their right mind would jump into the relationship cesspool after back-to-back failures? Ever the eternal optimist, I still held on to the *happily ever after fairytale romance* just like the next girl.

When we first met, Dan (Husband #3) and I spent hours on the phone—after all, we were in the early LUST phase—more on that later. With both former mates seeking lustier pastures, I was desperate for understanding, and he was a patient, albeit unconsciously conspiring, listener. During one lengthy rant, I lamented, "I just don't understand. One minute I was getting roses for my anniversary and the next, I was at the lawyer's office again! What the hell happened?"

This understanding man provided my first glimpse into the inner workings of the male psyche. His response? "It probably had less to do with love and more to do with LUST. Your previous partners probably did love you on an emotional level, but other forces may have been at work behind the zipper!"

Well, this was nothing revolutionary! I had spent enough time fending off the octopus-like arms of adolescent boys to know they were driven by sex. I also, incorrectly, expected as boys matured into men, sex would be only one of many reasons for a lasting relationship.

Apparently, I was wrong.

He continued, "A powerful urge for sex, driven by evolution and survival instincts, is one reason men stray."

"If a guy tells you he *never* looks at or lusts for other women— he's either lying or he's gay! LUST is a challenge, even a curse for the man who wants to remain faithful to his mate. When the lust wears off, the urge to mate with a new woman is strong," he suggested.

"Some guys act on it, some don't."

My reaction to his theory? Indignation and disgust! Acceptance of this kind of skewed logic would give men a free pass to be ultimate assholes. Their excuse? "It's biological, I can't help it!"

My emotional self yearned to believe the romance novels, soap operas, and love songs. But after two failed marriages, I was open to just about anything, even contemptible ideas like his.

When reality slaps you in the face, I guess it's easier to let go of fairytales.

Could this unorthodox explanation for male infidelity help me to understand my own checkered past and pave the way for another relationship when most would be swearing celibacy or changing sides? Oddly, it did help me feel better about myself.

I was certain there must be something horribly wrong with me for this to happen TWICE! As you read this, you may be thinking the same thing—she's probably a CRAZY bitch with some hidden, horrible traits. While you may get a very different story from my former mates, from *my* perspective, I was pretty normal.

Still, I vigorously questioned this radical idea. Was he just defending other men—like some sort of guy loyalty club—or was there hard evidence to support a theory that males are hard-wired to seek multiple sex partners as a way to ensure our lineage—even when it is socially unacceptable? There was more to it than even he realized.

It took years for me to apply his logic to my own relationship woes, but the honest, often uncomfortable dialogue did whet my appetite to prove or disprove his theory. After all, I was not only living with yet another male but I had spawned two sons of my own. I needed answers!

———————————————————

Should men be excused for centuries of sexual harassment, objectification, and subjugation of women because of a biological urge to mate? Absolutely NOT! Whacking off or taking a cold shower can, and should, easily take care of the "problem" without dehumanizing anyone!

Does my understanding of male lust mean that I support open relationships, allowing him to act on those biological urges? No. Do I think he is genetically predestined to cheat at some point? Not at all. If he is cheating, it is only in his fantasies, *as far as I know*. Right now, I enjoy the relationship we do have.

However, I am under no delusions that it could never happen to us, but for the time being—he is MY asshole and I am HIS bitch!

Are all men assholes and all women bitches all the time? There are those tender moments—just prior to, during, and immediately after sex—when we are closest to finding equilibrium. Enjoy the fleeting moments. They are all you are gonna get!

The 'Boner-Room'

3

Equal Time

When a man gives his opinion, he's a man. When a woman gives her opinion, she's a bitch.. ~Bette Davis

Guys aren't the only ones who struggle with fidelity, but the reasons are usually quite different. If biological LUST is a major cause of cheating in men, which can lead to being considered assholes, then lack of emotional intimacy—not a "wiener gone wild"—may be responsible for female infidelity. Men may want new snatch, but women just want attention and someone who will listen to them bitch!

In the beginning of any relationship, guys put on their "A" game to get what they really want—SEX! They will *appear* sensitive, writing sappy love poems or sending flowers, but let's face it, after awhile, a guy's idea of emotional intimacy is "how about a blow job, honey?"

So, what do many women do? They seek the arms of a sensitive, willing listener—someone who doesn't treat their commentary like the teacher in a Peanuts cartoon. Unfortunately, Mr. New Sensitivity is almost certainly no different than her current asshole! Do you think he is really interested in your bitching? Maybe, but only to the point where it gets him into your big girl panties!

There's nothing like the thrill of feeling attractive to someone other than the person staring at you across the breakfast table with bedhead or those electrifying sex-charged moments in a new relationship. Bombarded constantly with images of airbrushed goddesses on TV and in magazines, it is easy for women to feel insecure and unattractive—especially when you have applesauce in your hair and a kid on your hip. Not to mention, your mate has seen your stretch marks, smelled your farts, seen you with no makeup—in other words, experienced you at your worst.

Is it any wonder that some women fall victim to the attention of a new and different asshole?

A girl may lust for the perfectly toned body of an affectionate, new asshole; but after she wipes the drool from her chin, she is probably thinking "he has such kind eyes" or "wouldn't he make a great dad? He's so sensitive!"

Even with the temptation of a new guy, she often resists, comparing her "Adonis" at home to the new lust interest. She reasons, "This one's already housebroken!" The long-term asshole may still come out on top (both figuratively and eventually, literally). But not always.

Are all men assholes because of SEX? No. Are all women bitches because of SENSITIVITY and SECURITY? Of course, not. Yet, one thing is for certain, both sexes are faced with biologically based challenges that may cause them to act like bitches and assholes.

WOMEN'S ASS SIZE STUDY

There is a new study about women and how they feel about their asses. The results were pretty interesting: 30% of women think their ass is too fat....10% think their ass is too skinny..........The remaining 60% say they don't care, they love him, he's a good man, and they wouldn't trade him for the world.

~ Anonymous

4
The Curse

*"**Men**struation, **Men**opause, **Men**tal breakdowns. Ever notice that all women's problems seem to begin with* **MEN**? *~girlfromparis@tumblr.com*

If unsolicited erections are a male's curse, the female curse is most certainly the menstrual cycle. Unfortunately, *her* curse doesn't last a few minutes like an erection! Women are LUCKY to have a couple of good weeks each month where they don't feel like ripping their asshole's head off or melting into a puddle of tears. With pimple outbreaks that resemble Mt. Vesuvius getting ready to erupt; bloating that feels like Shamu, the whale, and cramps that can cause her to double over in agony; females are stuck each month with a demon lurking inside waiting for just the right—or wrong—moment to appear!

At least, a guy who gets the urge to merge can deal with those unwanted erections quickly, using a bit of handiwork!

Bleeding bitches have been blamed for every misfortune imaginable from crop failure to cloudy mirrors to curdled milk; even stormy weather. Men were so terrified of these monthly hemorrhaging chicks, women were often sent away from the village during "Shark Week". Maybe it was just an excuse to avoid the wrath of the Hormonal Housewife!

For a species who solved many mysteries of the universe, it sure took a LONG time for us to understand our own bodies! Incredibly, less than 200 years ago, doctors still didn't connect ovulation to the routine visits from "Aunt Flow"; believing, instead, the monthly bleeding was a way for women to dispose of surplus blood, or to cool a heightened emotional state. They got the heightened emotional state right, it just wasn't called PMS yet!

Is it any wonder we are still playing catch-up, if a mere 50 years ago, women were afraid to wash their hair at that time of the month for fear of developing the dreaded "hasty consumption"?

Is there some secret school where young men learn to lust?

The Other Curse

If monthly bouts with the "Girl Flu" are considered a woman's biological curse, then man's natural curse may be LUST.

A guy can be doing something he really enjoys—*other than sex*—but a scantily clad woman walks by, and suddenly, the reptilian part of his brain takes control. Dopamine (you could call it dopey-juice) floods the pleasure centers as his penis takes a trip to fantasy land.

His *grasp* on reality loosened; the unsolicited, surprise erections appear, leaving him in quite the predicament, with few socially acceptable options. Even a bumpy road may cause his shaft to stand at nearly full attention!

I had never considered lust to be a curse for men, but for those who want to remain faithful to their partner, I guess it could be!

Deep within our genetic code, the urge to merge is hormonal; designed to ensure the success of our species, just like the hormones that control menstruation in women.

This reality is not easy for women (including me!) to accept. Women love sex too, but they don't get derailed by every walking dick they see.

"Why can't men just get a grip and learn some self-control?" women often wonder. A statement like that made in reverse during PMS might cause the guy to get slapped senseless!

It all goes back to basic biology and evolution. Females are hard-wired to temper those urges. After all, she can't just go wandering off in search of sex with kids to care for. The desire for sex is like any other desire she may have; *important*, but not to the point where it controls her life.

So what's the difference between the male and female curses? Lust, and it's consequences, may threaten an entire relationship, while a woman's period may only threaten the health and well-being of the unlucky male who gets in her way!

Should a woman be called a bitch just because she is a hormonal train wreck each month?

The *real* bitch is the girl who uses the monthly cycle as an excuse to bust the balls of all men, not the woman who is a hot mess because he didn't notice her new dress when it was that time of the month.

Should a man be called an asshole for merely thinking about sex with another woman as long as he doesn't act on it?

The *real* asshole is the guy who uses the strong biological urges of males as an excuse to force himself on a woman or treat her like nothing but a sex object, not the guy who innocently wonders if the waitress is wearing chocolate-flavored underwear.

If men are *cursed* with lust, and women are *cursed* with a monthly, hormonal roller coaster—is it possible to ever get along? The first step is to learn more about our sexual and emotional selves.

It begins with the three S's: Sex, Security and Sensitivity.

— ··· — ··· — ··· — ··· — ··· —

The kind of face a woman finds attractive on a man will differ, depending on where she is at in her menstrual cycle. For example, if she is ovulating, she's attracted to men with rugged, masculine features. However, if she is menstrual or menopausal, she tends to be attracted to a man with duct tape over his mouth and a spear lodged in his chest while he is on fire.

~Anonymous

5

The Three S's

Sex is like math. You add the bed. Subtract the clothes. Divide the legs. And hope you don't multiply.

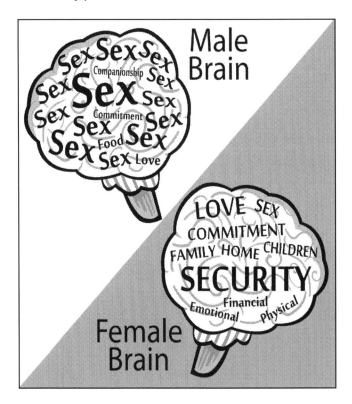

W hat *do* we want? Men want SEX and security. Women want SENSITIVITY, SECURITY and sex. After all, women are more complicated!

The roses he sent you for your birthday? Sex! He may actually be thoughtful and considerate, but if you are in the lust phase, you can bet his primary motivation is the SEX he hopes to receive for such sanctimonious gestures. Do you think he really is *dying* to drop $50 bucks on some pesticide-laden plants that will be dead in less than a week when he could have spent it at the golf course?

The sex she gave you for sending those roses? SECURITY. She actually may be into you but in the lust phase, what turns her on most may not be what you think. Looks are important, but a guy who is funny, *sensitive,* and also provides *security* for her and potential children—good husband material—is the one who turns her on the most. That hot sex is one way to keep you around, securing her place, at least till the LUST wears off.

But wait a minute! Women love sex and men want security or there would be nothing but one night stands! If we both want the same things, then what's the problem? It's all about how we are wired.

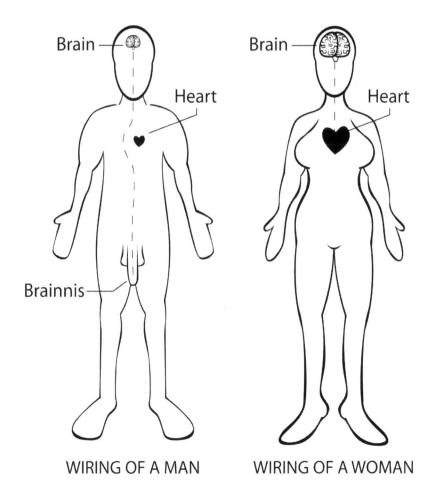

WIRING OF A MAN   WIRING OF A WOMAN

We know we are physically different—our boobs are different sizes; abundant facial hair versus little facial hair—at least until menopause kicks in—vaginas versus penises. Not only do we look differently, we think and act differently.

Feelings, Nothing More Than Feelings

From the woman who wears her heart on her sleeve to the high strung, defensive bitch—females are emotionally charged! As with Newton's Laws of Physics, all that emotion cannot be created nor can it be destroyed. It has to go somewhere, which often translates to the nearest object or person who gets in the wired woman's way. A sweet young lady can turn into a bitch on steroids or a blubbering bitch in seconds!

A girl can be in tears within minutes if her boyfriend says the right or wrong thing but the only way to bring most guys to tears is to kick them squarely in the family jewels!

For women, getting a guy to understand her feelings is almost as challenging as teaching him to put the toilet seat down! But we keep trying!

Are All Men Versions of Mr. Spock?

The emotionless male is immortalized in the Star Trek persona of Mr. Spock but if you think men are emotionless, you've never seen a bunch of guys watching the Super Bowl. There's plenty of emotion in that room!

What men really lack is SENSITIVITY! Call a guy an asshole and his response is "Go screw yourself!" or you might get punched in the face. Call a woman a bitch and her entire existence is under attack. *What do you mean by that? I thought you loved me!* Ironically, if a woman acts with less emotion—she's a bitch. A guy who is more sensitive, gets called a pussy! That's not much incentive for either of the sexes to change behavior.

Mr. Fix-It and The Mommy Mode

Men are natural born Mr. Fix-its. Try to talk to a guy about a problem and he immediately starts trying to fix the problem, even before a girl's rant is finished. While such gestures might be appealing, in the beginning, women don't want an emotional handyman. They just want someone to let them bitch—giving them time to think through their own solutions.

If a guy wants to rant about a problem, women automatically go into "Mommy" mode. *Oh, you have a boo-boo? Let mommy kiss it and make it all better.* The guy doesn't want his "boo-boo" kissed—maybe kissing another part of his anatomy would help but not by his mommy! Sex would make it all better; at least for a little while.

The need for SEX and SECURITY is shared among all animals. What complicates human relationships? SENSITIVITY—either too much or too little.

— .. — .. — .. — .. — .. — .. —

A wise ass once said…..nothing. He let her vent and they had sex afterward.

6

You Animal!

Women need a reason to have sex. Men just need a place. ~Billy Crystal

Why do we have such a hard time admitting we are members of the animal kingdom? We shave, wax or burn off every hair on our bodies trying to deny our mammalian selves. Yet, like it or not, we ARE animals with the same basic needs—food, shelter, and especially reproduction—all driven by instinct. Mention the word sex, and images of boobs and butts or penises and balls pop into our heads. But life's earliest forms didn't even have these basic parts, with sex relegated to a fusion of bodies—the first orgy?

Millions of years of evolution have created some bizarre forms and functions for living things to reproduce. Just imagine how different our sex lives might be if humans had evolved a detachable penis like the paper nautilus! *Honey, have you seen my penis? I know it was right here last night!* A lot of fumbling in the backseat of an old Chevy might have been avoided, if we had the prehensile penis of a tapir. That's like having another arm!

Big Boobs and Red Asses

We may not have detachable or prehensile penises, but in the path to humanity, our bodies have evolved, and some anthropologists believe it is, at least in part, due to SEX.

Those large fat-filled female breasts may be more than just extremely large milk jugs or a place for guys to bury their heads during a romp in the sack! Bigger boobs could be seen from farther away—like baboons with red asses—making it easier for our ancestors to find females. Since chasing after another guy to hump probably didn't end well, maybe it was survival of the *tittiest*.

The downward-tilting, female pelvis provided balance to walk upright for our early ancestors but there was a bonus to this natural selection! The forward tilt made the G-spot was easier to find and that meant multiple orgasms for the women. It's not surprising that these genes survived the test of time!

Sex-a-nomics

Ever wonder why women need all that foreplay to get their motor running while men are ready for sex at the drop of a hat?

It's just a matter of sex-a-nomics. Think about it. Sperm is cheap and eggs are expensive. Each ejaculation contains millions of sperm while a woman produces a grand total of 700-800 potential eggs in a lifetime! With millions of available sperm, a man can afford to share the love, while a woman, with a limited number of eggs, needs to invest wisely. She can't let just any dick fertilize this precious supply.

You would think that the overactive libido of males was responsible for human sexual evolution, but it may have actually been the female in the evolutionary driver's seat!

Most other mammals go into "heat" only once or twice a year and the rest of the time, they are celibate.

But not *Homo sapiens*! Sexy predecessors to our species, who were *willing* and *able* to get it on just about anytime, were rewarded by amorous males looking for a little release (okay, a lot of release) with more food and protection. With extra attention, these Lolitas of our ancestors were more likely to survive, raise young, and pass on those horny genes to us!

Matters of Size

Does size or appearance really matter? If it does, hooking up with a male barnacle would be like getting it on with John Holmes, of porn star fame, but the poor guy would need a 15-foot wagon to haul it around!

Men preoccupied with penis size can stand with pride when compared to the gorilla, close in body size (actually even larger) to humans, but a penis that would be an embarrassment to most males!

While we are on the subject of size, women are like Goldilocks. Not too large, not too small. Just right! A woman's needs are best met by a man who is attentive and can give her multiple orgasms not someone hung like a horse!

Guess Who's Coming For Dinner?

In the animal kingdom, mating rituals are as varied as the species themselves. Some animals even eat their mates after sex! Be glad you are not a male black widow spider or a praying mantis because you might be invited to dinner, only to discover, after sex, YOU are the main course!

What IS Normal?

Some fish can change sexes overnight and hermaphrodites, like the land snail, are both female and male. A few animals can even screw themselves and produce young. We wrongly assume sex is always about and between the same species of the opposite sex, resulting in offspring. Many believe homosexuality in humans is unnatural. But in the animal kingdom, homosexuality, along with many other human taboos, are everyday norms.

Believe it or not, biologists have observed over fifteen hundred species of animals having same sex attraction and practicing homosexual behavior. Hormonal and environmental factors can, and do, drive or inhibit reproductive strategies and sexual partner selection. When animal populations outpace the resources, guess what?

Some boy bunnies will only hump boy bunnies and not because of an over-domineering mother or by choice.

Disease, starvation, increasing predators, and yes, homosexuality, all help to reduce numbers of animals to a more balanced state. With our human population predicted to double by 2050, shouldn't we be embracing homosexuality, not demeaning it?

Animals also have sexual fetishes, masturbate, partake in oral sex, have sex with inanimate objects (orangutans make and use dildos of wood and bark), practice cross species sex (bestiality), sexual cannibalism (the female praying mantis will eat her mate after copulation), sexual prostitution, and even necrophilia (sexually frustrated male kakapo parrots of New Zealand have been filmed mating with dead seagulls). Eeeww! Talk about a double taboo!

So what's normal? In the animal kingdom, anything goes!

Mating For Life?

Are we really designed to be with just one sex partner for life like bald eagles or French angel fish? Even those who appear to be bonded for life are known to sneak some nookie on the side. The truth is you can't change basic biology—at least without surgery.

As members of the animal kingdom, our very life depends upon strong urges to mate and procreate. Just like our animal ancestors, males and females have evolved differently and to deny these differences is to deny our very nature.

Biology and instincts, shared with the rest of the animal kingdom, can explain the forms and functions of our bodies but when did we become assholes and bitches?

Some believe it all started in the Garden of Eden, but did it?

7

It All Started in the Garden (or Did It?)

The enemy is fear. We think it is hate; but it is fear. ~Ghandi

In the beginning, there was just Man and it was good. He was at peace with himself and nature. He could watch the birds and the bees without getting an erection. He was pure of thought. Then Woman came along and ruined everything. Man's pure untainted thoughts turned to lust and no longer did man think for himself but instead would be ruled by his penis! ~Anonymous male, sometime B.C.

The First Asshole?

God has to be a man! A woman would never blame the fall of mankind on another woman! EVE just wanted someone to understand her! Who ate the apple first? ADAM! Who really got the blame? A poor innocent snake! The real culprit was the throbbing one eyed serpent between Adam's legs. And so the real curse of mankind began—the curse of lust. ~Anonymous female, sometime B.C.

The Original Bitch?

Sex in the Stone Age was a lot like the 60's and 70's, with free love and communal living, men and women coexisted in relative harmony and equality.

Without possessions to cause conflict, even paternity didn't matter. With everyone helping, the village did raise the child.

Gender roles were blurred too. You might have found Sally with a spear and Sam in an apron! Exaggerated cartoons of cavemen, club in one hand, dragging a woman around by the hair in the other, have been replaced with a more likely scenario. Super sexy ladies who would screw just about anytime (not just in heat like other mammals), were really in control.

For both, it was a win-win situation. The male who provided food and security to his female partner could have all the nookie he wanted without battling other males or wandering around. With their bellies full and legs spread, these sex goddesses survived long enough to pass on their libido and social status. The Sex Contract was born and for millennia, women and men lived together equally.

Blame It On the Hoarder

But all that peace and love changed when we settled down and started growing food! Yes, food! Successful farmers became intoxicated by the heady effects of POWER. *I've got more food and land than you do! Wanna trade your sweet, sexy daughter for some of it?* The asshole was born! You can bet the birth of the bitch wasn't far behind. It's true that the SECURITY of marriage to a wealthy land owner would have been attractive to a woman but being traded like a chess piece must have created a lot of frustrated young bitches!

Did men and women become assholes and bitches because of one apple? More likely, it was the whole tree full of apples and the potential for wealth and power that came with it.

The first bitch wasn't Eve, but more likely, a frustrated girl in love with the poor shepherd down the road—not the old, unattractive land baron!

The Sex Contract, with women in control, was replaced with Marriage Contract by power-addicted men who were terrified of the seductive, alluring female. It was the beginning of the end for women.

The Fear Factor

Power is addicting, yet, here was a creature able to erase all the power and control men could muster with the wiggle of her hips or the wink of her eye!

Fear of the mystical female who could create life from between her loins, resulted in abominable practices by panicked, power-hungry males, like clitoral mutilation to prevent those multiple orgasms women enjoy (jealous, guys?), covering women from head to toe, or reducing them to subhuman status—and we have been suffering the consequences ever since. Attitudes are slowly changing, with more value today on brains than brawn, but it has been 10,000 years in the making!

Nothing is so powerful in drawing the spirit of a man downwards as the caresses of a woman. St. Augustine, 401 A.D.

8

Handfasting

Marriage is a wonderful institution—who wants to live in an institution?
~Groucho Marx

No, this chapter is not about whacking off, that *cums* later. Here, we explore the roots of marriage and monogamy.

If most, if not all, animals have sex with multiple partners to continue the species, why did we become monogamous? You may believe the practice of one man, one woman for eternity, or monogamy, comes directly from God. It doesn't. For centuries, and especially throughout the Old Testament, men had multiple wives.

It's the Romans who can take credit for the one wife policy before Christianity ever began, and it had nothing to do with love and everything to do with control. Romans, in their quest for power, needed warriors, but horny, young recruits with only one thing on their mind, were not easy to control.

Wealthy men could afford scores of wives and that meant a wife shortage. The poor soldier was left with his wanker in his hand and no where to put it.

The one wife policy, rich or poor, adopted by Augustus, solved the problem. With a steady supply of reliable sex, soldiers focused on the job at hand and went on to conquer.

Christianity took up where the Greeks and Romans left off, but not for the high moral reasons or theology you might imagine.

Priests, during the early days, were endowed with lots of land and a harem of wives who bore them scores of children. Believe it or not, as many as ten popes were married and had children prior to becoming Pope!

There was just one problem.

When the priests died, who inherited the land? The kids? Or the Church? Since land spelled power and wealth, the Church was reluctant to give up that control.

Pope Siricius, who left his wife to become Pope, declared it a sin for priests to sleep with their wives. No nookie, no offspring, no problem! Well, not quite. This unnatural containment of sexual desire would later lead some men of the cloth down a pathway of repulsive behavior.

If a priest was not allowed to have any sex, then certainly, the parishioners should not be allowed to ENJOY it! The Council of Trent in the 16th century proclaimed virginity and celibacy to be the holiest of holy, even superior to marriage. Sex was demonized as sin and only to be used to produce children, certainly not for pleasures of the flesh!

Priests, monks, and nuns were left to deal with these natural urges by resorting to masturbation (also considered a sin) or the extreme sacrifice—castration— to calm the fires of desire.

Handfasting

Even the traditional marriage vows of today are rooted, not in the divine, but in POWER and GREED. In 16th century Scotland, people "claimed" to be married in order to secure land and possessions. With no way to verify these unions, the practice of *handfasting* was born. Since the Church was both the civil and moral authority, couples were required to seal the deal in front of a priest by holding hands, making it a legally binding contract. Once again, the revered ceremony had little to do with morality, and more to do with possessions.

Serial Monogamists

In Western cultures, most of us still aspire to strict monogamy—one man and one woman till death do us part—but it is not making perfect! With the divorce rate at nearly 50%, at least half of us have had multiple mates (I have legally had three!). If you count pre-marital sex partners and cheating—we are really *serial monogamists*—one partner at a time, but multiple sex partners throughout a lifetime. Just like the rest of the animal kingdom, perhaps serial monogamy is indeed buried deep within our DNA.

All Shacked Up

In the not so distant past, your parents would disown you if you moved in with your love (or lust interest) but shacking up is the new normal for many couples today. "Why buy the cow when you can get the milk for free?" is now "Why buy a car without test driving it first?" While some think shacking up is the root of moral decline in our country, others see it as an insurance policy. But one thing seems certain. The days of the virgin bride are slipping away. Are we just following the call of the wild?

It's all in the DNA!

Relationships are like a box of
chocolates.
The outside always looks
scrumptious.
While the inside is always
an uncertainty.

~Dan Dourson~

9

The Mating Game

Love is blind? No. Love is clarity. Lust is blind. ~Dan Dourson

From the moment we emerge from the womb, we are bombarded from all sides with sex! Just ask any ad executive. Sex sells! This constant brainwashing can be almost impossible for an innocent young mind to ignore. What do we get in return? A lot of misguided young assholes and bitches with unrealistic expectations!

Gushy love songs, teen magazines, or romance novels full of torrid love scenes that send your heart and libido racing continue the myths of romance for hormone-charged teeny boppers that linger through to adulthood. Metaphors to the male orgasm like "an explosion of hot fire" are a far cry from the fumbling in the back seat of a car. Is it any wonder young girls become frustrated bitches?

Caught between a rock and a *hard* place, peer pressure to "score", along with expectations from the girl to act like one of the main characters in a romantic comedy, can be prime breeding grounds to transform innocent, young men into heartless assholes.

Laws of Attraction

The mating game is all about attraction. Frogs use calls, birds use song, dance, and feathers. Human females teeter on shoes built like stilts and stand shivering in skimpy dresses, waiting for a table on Valentines Day. Males spend hours working out or buy flashy cars.

The laws of attraction might seem random, but they are anything but random! Whether animal or human, all have the same thing in mind—SEX! But not just any partner will do. Just like other animals—we are choosy. Our standards may lower out of desperation, but most of the time, if we hook up at all, there is usually a physical attraction.

So what is attractive?

Big booty babes sturdy enough to handle the rigors of childbirth might have been the hot mamas in the past, but today, anorexic-looking models set the standard. Intellectual types like Bill Gates or funny guys like Jim Carey are just as attractive now as butt-kicking Chuck Norris-types.

The laws of attraction are more than just big boobs and butts or a chiseled frame and movie star looks. Fortunately, attraction is highly subjective—it could be the curve of the face, the color of the hair, the size of the butt or the muscles, the smile, or the scent. Regardless of the initial attraction, mating rituals—from the most primitive tribes of Aborigines to the socialites of New York City—are virtually the same.

It all begins with the flirt and that starts with the eyes.

The soul, fortunately, has an interpreter - often an unconscious but still a faithful interpreter - in the eye. ~ Charlotte Brontë, Jane Eyre

The commentary describing the mating ritual of humans might go something like this:

"And here we observe the female of the species as she initiates the mating game. A lift of the brow, then a wide-eyed gaze, and finally, a coy eyelid drop. With a quick tilt, then drop of her head, and a glance to the side, she coyly makes eye contact. The male of the species, initiates his flirt with his chest thrust outward and hands behind his head. This posture communicates receptiveness. But it will get him nowhere if the target female ignores him!"

The mating game continues with the **approach,** which is all about signals and cues. *Did she really smile at me or was it the guy next to me? Do I take a chance and risk getting rejected immediately?* The distance across the room can seem like a football field, as he, or more recently, she, makes the approach. But the risk is still the same.

Rejection or acceptance?

Next comes the **small talk.** Attraction can quickly turn to repulsion if her voice is a high pitched shrill like fingernails on a chalkboard or he sounds like Alvin or the Chipmunks! The person, who was mesmerizing seconds before, is now a total turnoff!

Finally, there is the **casual touch.** That first skin to skin contact may feel like 120 volts of electricity surging through your body if there is a love connection or it might cause you to recoil in disgust if there is not!

If you make it past this final stage of the flirt, you are headed full speed ahead to the LUST phase.

The Lust Phase

It often gets labeled "Falling in Love". We disagree. It's not falling in LOVE—a much deeper, cerebral emotion that involves long term commitment and attachment—it's falling in LUST! When you fall in LUST, all common sense goes out the window, replaced, instead, with complete and total idiocy.

We all remember it. Guys hold farts, squelch the belch, and resist the urge to rearrange their "junk" in front of her. Girls wouldn't dream of pulling stray facial hair in front of him (a personal "favorite" of my husband), squeezing a zit or taking while he shaves. We avoid all the inevitable unpleasantries of daily life as if they do not exist for fear of frightening off the new lust interest.

"Could this be THE ONE...this awesome asshole?" girls wonder. "Do I really have a shot at this beautiful bitch?" guys fantasize.

A guy in LUST becomes unrecognizable to friends, catering to the newest woman's every whim.

"Let's go shopping all day then watch reruns of Sex in the City" she suggests. "Oh, that sounds like fun!" he lies.

Normally sexual sprinters—men will proclaim "it's more about you than me", treating the lady to a long, passionate night of multiple orgasms.

A girl in LUST will wear a thong that feels like dental floss between her cheeks, when what really she really wants is to put on a pair of comfy, granny panties. She will laugh at his crude jokes, tolerate his disgusting friends, and pretend to really care about his latest hobby, even if it is underwater basket-weaving!

Then, there's oral sex. Do men really think women like putting their mouths where they have just taken a whiz?

With your head in the clouds or up someone's ass, the lust phase cannot be sustained. One day, you may wake up and realize, the traits you deemed "cute" in the beginning or habits like her smoking or his slovenly ways, now annoy the hell out of you!

The hot sex on the kitchen table is replaced with the routine sex of Saturday nights.

As the LUST phase winds down, so does the dopamine that surges to our brains. Luckily, another powerful chemical, oxytocin—takes over where dopamine left off, and triggers a cuddle and bond response (isn't that what women want?).

Oxytocin is so effective, it's been used with autistic patients! But is the increase in oxytocin enough to sustain and maintain a monogamous relationship? In some cases, yes, in others, no. It all depends upon the person.

What was once torrid and steamy becomes secure and soothing, with passion found in living life with a committed partner, not just in sex. The LUST is replaced with LOVE and that's the real glue that binds.

From Lust to Love

When the romance gives way to everyday routines, women may discover they are nothing more than a maid or mommy replacement. Men may find themselves in the role of a little boy, controlled by a mommy-figure.

Women wonder, "What happened to that sensitive, sweet guy?" He fell out of lust! Out of frustration and disillusionment, women become BITCHES!

Men wonder, "What happened to that sexy, hot babe I married?" Out of disillusionment and frustration, men become ASSHOLES!

The couples who make it to the love phase and beyond, still seek passion in their lives with new, stimulating experiences: a hobby, a new job, new friends, travel, even alternative sex positions and role-playing—or *writing a book about bitches and assholes*!

If you can replace that savage passion with passion for life itself, you have the best chance to sustain and maintain a relationship for years to come.

The Soulmate Lottery

The word *soulmate* is passed around these days like a 95-cent hooker. How many times have you heard "I found my soulmate" and six months later, that person is gone? With billions of people on the planet, your perfect soulmate may live in Russia or the Amazon rainforest and the chances of finding that person is unlikely.

What the hell is a soulmate anyway? Some say it's someone just like you; others believe it's someone completely opposite. If a **soul** is defined as a *spirit* and a **mate** is somebody you *screw*, then a soulmate is your *spiritfucker*! I could have ended up with any number of *spiritfuckers*—and *did* end up with two others—and still been just as happy.

If you find someone who doesn't gross you out when you look at them, or make you cringe when they speak; who doesn't put you down, but helps you grow as a person—maybe, that person is your soulmate—at least, for now.

The mating game is just that. It is a crapshoot or a spin of the roulette wheel—thrilling, if you are winning, but, oh so frustrating, if you are not! You can never be guaranteed to have a lifelong relationship with one individual. From LUST to LOVE; is it still worth the risk?

From Lust   **To Love**

10
Rate Your Date Before You Mate

Nobody likes getting dumped. But the chances of staying together today are no better odds than a coin toss, and yet, we still keep on trying! The demise of a relationship is often one of the most painful experiences we encounter. Who wants to be on a pain roller coaster for a lifetime?

What if there were ways to *rate your date before you mate*?

From the scientific to the silly, this section will have you whipping out a tape and measuring your fingers to see what secrets they may reveal.

Use the Bitchometer and Asshole Assessment to rate the assholes and bitches in your life or see where you stand. Finally, read the results of our unscientific poll to learn….what is the Perfect Man or Perfect Woman?

Divulging Digits

Have you ever wished you could skip the pleasantries and cut right to the chase even BEFORE the first date? The answer may be in the palm of the hand!

Imagine a dating world, where along with a condom (just in case), your date brings a tape, and subtly begins to measure your fingers or online dating websites that request your 2D:4D ratio as part of your profile.

What's a 2D:4D ratio? It's a physical record of testosterone and estrogen exposure by a fetus before its even born, written in the lengths of your index and ring fingers.

The emerging secrets are nothing less than staggering. From penis length to autism to sexual orientation and more, the 2D:4D ratio is not just a way to avoid hooking up with the wrong girl or guy, it could be the next non-invasive way to diagnose a host of medical conditions!

You think that's bizarre? Believe it or not, women's finger lengths actually change slightly during her monthly cycle. Fingers that change lengths? That's like something out of a horror movie!

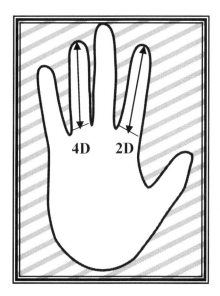

To find your 2D:4D ratio:

- Measure the length of your index finger from the crease where your finger joins your palm to the tip.

- Do the same with your ring finger.

- Divide the index finger number by the ring finger number. Voila! You have your 2D:4D ratio!

Penis Length, Autism and Sexual Orientation—Oh MY!

What do these seemingly unrelated subjects have in common? They can all be determined by your 2D:4D ratio! What do your digits divulge about you?

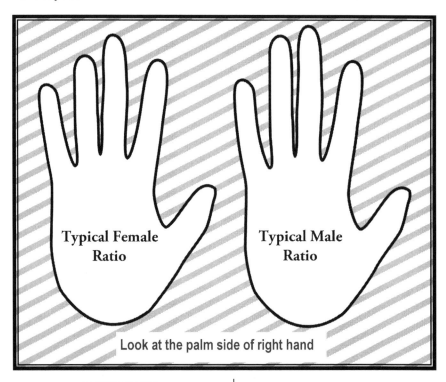

Typical Female Ratio

Typical Male Ratio

Look at the palm side of right hand

HIGHER RATIO: INDEX IS THE SAME OR LONGER THAN RING FINGER	LOWER RATIO: INDEX IS SHORTER THAN RING FINGER
~Shorter penis length ~Higher pitch voice ~Higher fidelity ~Less aggressive ~Verbal ~ Gay and male-to-female transgender ~Asymmetrical faces ~Lower risk for alcoholism ~Males increased incidence of prostate cancer	~Longer penis length ~More likely to cheat ~More aggressive ~Deeper pitch voice ~Better athletic performance ~Higher scores on medical school entrance exams ~Lesbians and female-to-male transgender ~Higher incidence of Autism ~Symmetrical faces

The Quest For Zest

Super-Sale $19.95

Having problems getting it up? For the low price of just $19.95, we guarantee the animal-tested product **"HARD-ON"** to work as well as any aphrodisiac on the market today. *This is our pledge to your feeble libido.* For additional product information on this amazing dysfunctional remedy, visit our website at www.**HARD-ON.cum**!

BITCH-O-METER

Bitches can go from Babe to Bitch in 60 seconds. What kind of bitch is she TODAY?

UNINTENTIONAL BITCH is mostly sunny and pleasant. She only gets bitchy during her monthly cycle and even then, she apologizes for it. She will never be an Ultimate Bitch. The worst thing the Unintentional Bitch will do is occasionally whine or gripe and maybe gossip a bit. While she is easy to be around, she is almost too easy-going. There will be times when you want to say, *"just get mad and BITCH about something!"*

VOLCANIC BITCH will rarely reveal her displeasure with you or anyone but under the surface there is a seething volcano of bitchiness that lies dormant waiting to erupt. She may live her whole life without a true explosion but if her bitchiness ever makes it to the surface, LOOK OUT! You do not want to be anywhere around when all that pent up frustration bursts forth.

CLUELESS BITCH has no idea that she is a bitch. When told that her comments are mean or hurtful, she honestly cannot understand how anyone could think that she is being bitchy. She will get offended if anyone dares to call her a bitch and may go into bitch overdrive. The extreme Clueless Bitch will be one of the more challenging to live with. Proceed with caution.

BITCH-IN-CHARGE is self-assured without busting your balls. She takes charge without being a control freak. She can be difficult to live with sometimes but it is worth it. Her self-confidence and self-assurance is downright sexy. Her bitchiness will help her succeed in life for she knows what she wants and gets it. This is the bitch that all men should aspire to call their own.

WANNABE BITCH hangs out with other true bitches like the BORN BITCH or ULTIMATE BITCH but will apologize when the true bitches say or do something mean. She needs to find nicer friends and stop pretending she is a true bitch when she's not.

ALL TALK, NO ACTION BITCH constantly threatens to "break out a can of whoop-ass" while backing up. She talks a big game but in reality will do whatever it takes to avoid confrontation. This type of bitch will get you into trouble with very large biker guys or other bitches.

BORN BITCH came out of the womb that way. Her earliest signs of bitchiness emerge in preschool when she takes everyone's toys while smiling sweetly. This kind of bitch cannot blame her bitchiness on the time of the month or a crappy childhood. She was genetically predestined to be a bitch and she really can't help it. She will most likely mature into a Clueless Bitch or an Ultimate Bitch.

OCCASIONAL BITCH is the other type that men should pursue. Like the Unintentional Bitch and the Bitch-in-Charge, she gets bitchy during that time of the month OR when situations call for a bitch; like encounters with the *Ultimate Bitch* or the *All Talk No Action Bitch*. She can hold her own against these bitches but rarely directs her bitchiness at males (only ones who cheat on her).

UPTIGHT BITCH acts like she has a permanent carrot shoved up her ass. She is judgmental and critical of everyone around her. Like the Ultimate Bitch, she believes her viewpoint is always correct and yours is always wrong. She can't relax and laugh at herself or others. She is too busy judging everyone and worrying about what everyone else will think to relax and have fun and she will find this book obnoxious.

ULTIMATE BITCH has no regard for anyone else's feelings and doesn't care what she says or does. She must be the center of attention at any social event and do ANYTHING for attention (including causing a scene). She will tell you she is madly in love with you and then sleep with your best friend. She really believes she is always right. If you dare blame her for anything, she will twist the truth to make her the victim and everyone else look bad. She has few friends because even other bitches can't tolerate her except the Wannabe Bitches. The intoxicating aura of this bitch often ensnares many unsuspecting men until it is too late. These unfortunate guys spend many hours wondering how and why they ended up with the Ultimate Bitch!

ASSHOLE ASSESSMENT

Assessing his level of assholeness before sex is nearly impossible. The statements <u>during</u> and <u>after</u> sex are the most revealing. If you haven't been intimate yet, read the 5 statements BEFORE SEX only.

Answer TRUE or FALSE.

BEFORE SEX:

1. He talks on the phone with you for hours.
2. He always pays, opens doors, and pulls out your chair.
3. He hangs on your every word with "lust"-struck eyes.
4. He seems to love shopping for hours.
5. He never farts, scratches his balls, pick his nose or belches in front of you.

If you have two or more FALSE *answers,* DO NOT SLEEP WITH THIS ASSHOLE! If you already have, proceed to the next sets of statements.

....

DURING SEX:

1. He's quick to come and slow to satisfy.
2. He brags about his performance. *I'm the best you have ever had, right?*
3. His idea of foreplay is getting head.
4. In the heat of passion, he screams somebody else's name.
5. After HIS climax, but not necessarily yours, he's reaching for the remote.

AFTER SEX:

6. He flirts with other women in front of you.
7. He cancels your next date to "go out with the guys" and hooks up with someone new.
8. He talks about nothing but himself.
9. He hates talking on the phone, shopping, and your friends.
10. He doesn't act like he did before sex—until he's horny again (this is a big one ladies).

ASSHOLE SCORE CARD

Count the number of TRUE answers to the 10 statements DURING and AFTER sex. Use the rating scale below to decide if he is worth your time.

0	True	**MR. PERFECT ASSHOLE** He's PERFECT. But careful, If it seems to good to be true, it probably is.
1	True	**KEEPER ASSHOLE** He likely the best chance for a lasting relationship.
2-4	True	**OKAY ASSHOLE** He may not be your dream guy but keeps your bed worm at night.
5-7	True	**BARELY TOLERABLE ASSHOLE** You should only continue dating him until something else better comes along. Don't feel bad about stringing him along. He deserves it.
8-10	True	**ULTIMATE ASSHOLE** Walk, no—run as fast as you can away from this asshole. Don't give him a thought or waste your time unless you want to be used then dumped at a later date.

Is the perfect mate out there? We asked a few friends and some random people on the street—*what is your idea of the perfect man or woman?*

THE
PERFECT MAN
From a female's point of view

Strong, muscular, brave, funny,
intelligent, witty, sensitive, intuitive,
cunning, caring, nurturing,
gregarious, hard-working,
fun-loving, alert, aware, protective,
supportive, encouraging,
thoughtful, financially secure,
spontaneous, attentive,
adventuresome, kind, sympathetic,
understanding, helpful,
compassionate, inspiring, confident, cheerful,
conscientious, polite,
devoted, rational, sensible, wise,
entertaining, perceptive, shrewd,
insightful, affectionate, devoted,
successful, inventive, resourceful,
creative, ingenious, clever, stimulating, motivat-
ing, gentle, kindhearted,
charming, eager, engaging,
prosperous, well-mannered,
sophisticated, naughty but not too naughty, risk
-taker, intellectual.......

Not too much to ask, right ladies?

THE
PERFECT WOMAN
From a male's point of view

11

The ~~Seven~~-Year Itch

When asked why all her marriages failed, Margaret Mead replied, "I have been married three times and not one of them was a failure."

The relationship road is filled with potholes. From lust to love to divorce, whole careers in therapy have been made or broken, attempting to explain what makes couples succeed or fail.

I wish I could offer a better outlook, but the truth is, even though we tend to be serial monogamists—one partner at a time—we may be pre-destined by evolution to flirt, fall in lust, mate, produce young, separate, and start the whole thing over again, especially when we are at the peak of our reproductive years. Is wanderlust hardwired in humans to survive?

The Seven-Year Itch?

From the tribes of the Amazon to the socialites of New York, no culture seems immune to what was once called the Seven-Year Itch. Popularized in a movie from the 1960's, the Seven-Year Itch chronicles the inevitable wandering eye and infidelity may occur, somewhere around the seventh year in many relationships. Those itchy feet may actually be part of our survival strategy.

Early in our history, it was common for couples to hook up, have a kid, stay together long enough for it to survive without the help of both parents, then split. The whole process took about four years or the Four-Year Itch. males started looking for someone new to accept their DNA, just in case, and women were also on the hunt for new genetics so their kids would have the best chance to live.

In the modern world, couples may not have children right away, so really the Itchy Feet Syndrome could occur anywhere from four to seven years after the initial hookup. Come to think of it, my past relationships did begin to disintegrate as the lust phase was wearing off, between the third and fourth year. I guess my once-endearing little quirks began to fester into oozing seeping boils that needed to be lanced and my mates felt that strong urge to seek a new partner.

The urge to wander might be "wired" into our DNA, but it doesn't mean that EVERYONE is destined to divorce. We all know of couples who remain happily married throughout long lifetimes together—without resorting to hacking off body parts, the use of straightjackets, or Valium. Our hats off to those who have beaten the odds!

— ·· — ·· — ·· — ·· — ·· — ·· — ···

Men are born between a woman's legs.
They spend the rest of their lives trying
to get back between them.
Why?
Because there's no place like
home!

12

The Quest for Zest

Aphrodisiacs are for those men who lack the balls to accept the inevitable.
~Dan Dourson

Getting ready for a hot date? When you splash on cologne or perfume, you may be unwittingly spraying yourself with whale feces! Ambergris, a concoction of indigestible squid beaks or other disgusting stuff from the intestines of a sperm whale, is one of the main ingredients in some of the most expensive, well-known brands of perfume and cologne in the world! Competition among hunters of this gross elixir of love is so fierce. some risk life and limb to collect $20 a gram or $9,000 a pound.

Human body odor, a huge turn-off to most of us today, may have been the first aphrodisiac. When I first met Dan, he had the unusual habit of sniffing the crease between my nose and cheek, because he said it smelled like me. At least it wasn't my armpit! I thought it was weird at the time, but I guess he was attracted to my natural musk!

If you think whale shit for perfume is disgusting, be glad you didn't live in 17th century Germany, where men drank menstrual blood to increase their libido. If that doesn't turn your stomach, imagine a cocktail made from the mixture of oil, wine, and the excrements of pigeons, snails, and toads to improve sexual performance.

Remember when you were a preteen and everything resembled genitalia or any comment could have a sexual connotation? In the absence of science, men have been proverbial preteens (and, often, still are) when trying to get and maintain an erection. If a plant or animal part looked like a penis, testicle, or vagina, then it should help a guy maintain a stiffy, or so the logic went.   Plants like Ginseng, or "manroot" are still used for sexual enhancement.

The poor rhino has the unfortunate luck of having a horn that resembles an erect penis (well, sort of). Superstition and a lack of knowledge has decimated and desecrated majestic creatures, all in the name of curing LDS (Limp Dick Syndrome). Powdered rhino horn was rumored to give a guy the ability to have sex all night long.

In the quest for zest, males share the bulk of the responsibility for the atrocities committed, in an attempt to regain the virility of youth.

You are not likely to find women chasing after rhino horns or tiger penises in search of the big O! That can easily be achieved with a few AA batteries and a good vibrator

Other outlandish treatments to enhance and increase male sex drive like a substance dubbed Spanish fly— derived from blister beetles—may actually promote an erection, just through basic chemistry, but overconsumption of this substance can result in death![7] Quite a chance to take just to get a boner!

Throughout history, humans have spent countless hours and enormous amounts of energy to enhance or maintain a sexual experience. Ironically, an equal amount of time and effort has been devoted to the suppression of the same desires; including the creation of that familiar breakfast food, corn flakes.

13

If You Don't Stop That, You'll Go Blind

"If God had intended us not to masturbate, He would have made our arms shorter." ~George Carlin

Her legs wrapped around the steel pole of the jungle gym and her vagina pressed up against the bar, a young girl's first sexual experience often occurs in an unlikely place, the school playground. What was that amazing sensation? Too young to understand this new found delight, she only knows that she wants to feel it again, so up the pole she goes. The first pole dance?

Fascination with the penis begins as soon as the young male gets control over arm and hand movements. As he pulls and tugs on this odd-looking appendage, a strange and wonderful sensation wafts over him. He won't know till much later what it is or why, but it feels good! The beginning of CTS or Carpal Tunnel Syndrome?

Our puritanical roots caused many of us to think it was wrong, sinful, and for some, a *mortal* sin to masturbate. Yet, it is the cleanest, safest form of sexual expression we have!

If pleasuring yourself is so wrong, then why do a wide variety of animals routinely practice it with paws, feet, flippers, and fingers?[1] Even young male wild turkeys, outwitted by older toms and left out during mating season, have been filmed masturbating with a cow pie in the middle of a field. With no chance of passing on genetics associated with animal sex, animals must do it because it feels good!

A Bad Rub

For centuries, this pleasurable act has been demonized and blamed for all sorts of problems from stunted growth to hairy palms to blindness. *If you don't stop that you'll go blind!*

Appalling as it sounds, children were placed in straightjackets at bedtime to prevent this innocent, healthy outlet for a purely biological urge! Women and men were forced to wear to chastity belts and "junk controllers"—a spiked male chastity belt.

"The Junk Controller"

We weren't always so uptight about masturbation. Graffiti found on cave walls depicted scenes of males and females, unashamedly in the act. The "juices of life" were believed to contain magical powers. Pharaohs and rulers would even jack off in public rituals to show authority. Glad I missed that era!

Egyptians believed the ebb and flow of the Nile, the longest river in the world, was controlled by the ejaculations of one of their Gods. He must have been a real regular!

Ancient Greeks thought masturbation was a safety valve against destructive sexual frustration. I guess the priests and nuns a few centuries later didn't get that memo.

One ancient myth turned out to be true. According to legend, a man who masturbated had a better chance of fathering a child. Guess what? It's true! Jacking off helps get rid of older, less viable sperm, making room for a fresh, new batch!

And that's not all. Women who masturbate before sex improve the chances of getting pregnant. Imagine a fertility clinic of the future where the doctors "prescribe" masturbation!

It might even help prevent cancer. A guy who empties his prostate once a week—with or without a partner—is less likely to develop prostate cancer!

The act of self-pleasure, once considered to be the root of all evil, should be considered a remedy instead! .

So pull those vibrators out and put the lotion to the motion!

Corn Flakes and Graham Crackers

Did you have a bowl of corn flakes for breakfast this morning? If you did, thank the puritanical Dr. John Kellogg's obsession with sexual repression! Corn flakes were invented by the prudish Dr. Kellogg who erroneously believed the consumption of grains would calm the fires of desire!

Convinced all human maladies were caused by sex, his horrific treatments included the use of carbolic acid on the clitoris to prevent female masturbation and orgasm. This medical monster was so uptight about sex, he remained celibate, marrying but never consummating his marriage.

Those delicious graham crackers we all ate as kids? They were created by Mr. Graham who also thought that grains would surpress sexual desire. Who would have ever guessed that graham crackers might have been part of a hidden agenda designed to curb the urges to slide down poles or climb ropes before we ever reached puberty?

Carpal Wrist

While Dr. Kellogg and Mr. Graham were inventing foods in order to curb masturbation and sexual desire, ironically, doctors in Europe were using vaginal massage or masturbation, to "cure" hysteria (translation: menopause or PMS) in women. The poor physicians performing this "procedure" soon developed carpal wrist which lead to the invention of the vibrator! Women everywhere are eternally grateful for their sacrifice!

A *Tug* of War

Thanks to the sexual revolution of the 1970's, masturbation has been upgraded from a mortal sin to an acceptable, safe way to deal with sexual desire in most circles. Vibrators and other sex toys are purchased in home "hen" parties by all ages of women, who blushingly purchase the model of their choice behind closed doors, then feverishly run to the nearest convenience store for batteries.

I guess stroking your own monkey seems more socially responsible than straightjackets or clitoral mutilation! Masturbation is a safe way for males to deal with the curse of lust and still maintain a monogamous relationship. Maybe it's better to marry a **beater** than a **cheater**.

Humans have been engaged in a sexual tug-of-war for centuries with aphrodisiacs and sexual enhancements on one side and devices of sexual repression on the other. The out "cum" remains to seen.

M
AS
TURB
ATION
DOESNT
SCREW
WITH
YOUR
EYES
HEALTH

14

Hall of Shame:
The Greatest Bitches and Assholes

"Nearly all men can stand adversity, but if you want to test a man's character, give him power." ~ Abraham Lincoln

No book about assholes and bitches would be complete without the recognition of those noteworthy individuals who have affected the course of human history as the greatest Assholes or Bitches. The largest thorns in our proverbial sides; the levels to which they have descended in order to gain power, control, sex, or security is almost beyond comprehension. While us mere mortals would be highly offended to be included in the Hall of Shame, many nominees may secretly consider inclusion to be an honor like an Academy Award for Asshole or Bitches.

You might expect the nominees to be the most despicable and despised throughout history; yet, many of our greatest inventors, scholars, poets, musicians, authors, actors, teachers, philosophers, leaders, and politicians are some of the most reviled or revered persons in history. The intoxicating affects of power can infect even those who begin with good intentions.

Hall of Shame Qualifications

What constitutes a place in this hallowed hall? It could be one horrendous bitchy or asshole act that transcends all decency and morality or a nominee may have been a consistent asshole or bitch throughout a lifetime.

Must someone be famous in order to be placed in the Hall of Shame? Of course not! In fact, our list is not considered comprehensive at all and should be considered highly subjective. You may not agree with the nominees we have selected.

In that case, there is space to nominate your own asshole and bitch recipients to the Hall of Shame. Who knows? You might even be dating a future recipient right now!

Selecting the "honorees" for the Hall of Fame was no easy task and the list is by no means exhaustive. No doubt you will think of others who may be more deserving.

ASSHOLE HALL OF SHAME

COPYCAT ASSHOLE   **Thomas Edison**
Credited with numerous inventions and the holder of thousands of patents, Tom was well known to have taken credit for others ideas. Proof that not ALL men are assholes because of sex.

DEMENTED ASSHOLE   **Dr. John Kellogg**
The inventor of the famous breakfast cereal, thought sex was responsible for all evil in the world. He prescribed horrific "treatments" like the use of carbolic acid on the clitoris to prevent female masturbation.

AXIS OF EVIL ASSHOLE   **Dick Chaney**
This sneaky asshole and his company Halliburton profited millions off the invasion and destruction of Iraq all under the auspices of national security. More like security of his own interests.

CONTRADICTORY ASSHOLE   **Thomas Jefferson**
Our revered founding father, professed freedom for all, but was the largest slave holder in the land. He believed slaves were not even people yet he bedded one and had numerous children by her.

CARELESS ASSHOLE   **Bill Clinton**
A careless asshole who should have kept his snake in his trousers or at least shot his wad into a paper towel not on a dress.

IMPOSTER ASSHOLE   **Christopher Columbus**
Columbus convinced himself and everyone else that he "discovered" the New World. In reality, he was a brutal dictator and slave trader who is also credited with bringing syphilis back to Europe and its rapid spread.

GREEDY ASSHOLE   **Bernie Maddoff**
A greedy asshole who had all anybody would need but wanted more and was willing to cheat millions of innocent poor people to achieve this goal.

FOX IN THE HEN-HOUSE ASSHOLE   **Anthony Weiner**
I believe I would have changed my last name. It became a little too prophetic. This asshole was on a committee dealing sexual abuse but was caught exposing himself on internet sites.. Watch out for the fox in the hen house.

BITCH HALL OF SHAME

COLD-BLOODED BITCH   **Bonnie Walker**

Bonnie (of Bonnie and Clyde fame) notorious for brutal acts on their nation-
wide crime spree. This is one bitch that you would not have wanted to encoun-
ter!

FICTIONAL SOUTHERN BITCH   **Scarlett O'Hara**

Even though Scarlett was a fictional character, Margaret Mitchell, who wrote
the epic, Gone with The Wind, captured the essence of the spoiled southern
bitch of the Civil War period.

CLUELESS BITCH   **Sarah Palin**

She came a little too close to having her finger on the "red" button, all while
remaining clueless about most things, including basic geography.

SHREWD BITCH   **Hillary Clinton**

She sucked it up and put on a happy face while her husband cavorted with
young interns and cigars. But she shrewdly toughed it out and has gone on to
be come a political force to reckon with in her own right.

OUTSPOKEN BITCH   **Rosanne Barr**

Rosanne became a household name with her no-holds-barred stand-up routine.
Our hats off to Rosanne for her contribution to women's empowerment and
opening the door for women to speak out.

ALLURING BITCH   **Elizabeth Taylor**

A perfect example of the serial monogamist with a total of seven marriages in
her lifetime, Liz had an allure that mesmerized even the most logical of men.
She was the kind of bitch who used her sex appeal to get what she wanted. Sev-
en times!

SELF-ABSORBED BITCH   **Lindsey Lohan**

Ms. Lohan began her young life as an innocent child star but her conduct as
an adult has left most of us with our heads shaking as she continues to live of a
life with little regard for those around her.

THE DO-IT-YOURSELF
BITCH & ASSHOLE
HALL OF SHAME

Did we miss someone you think is more deserving?

Here's your chance to give credit where credit is due by nominating your own candidates for the Bitch and Asshole Hall of Shame.

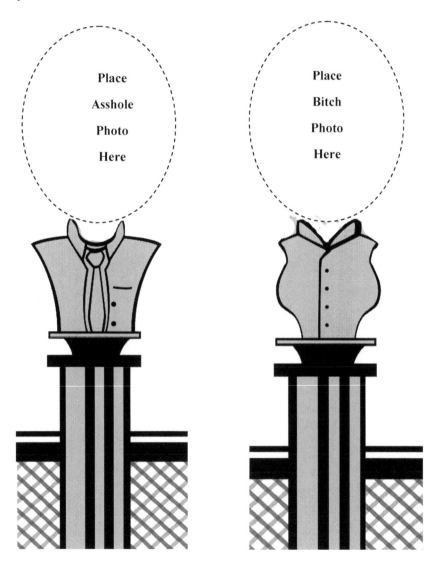

15

Sidesplitting Solutions

What is it that we really want? Companionship, love, relationships and sex.

The balance we seek may only be an illusion. Even nature is never entirely in a state of equilibrium.

If balance is but an illusion, why waste time worrying about the bitch and asshole dilemma? Here's some sidesplitting solutions like the *Jerky Hut* or *Love Potion #9* to give you a few laughs, instead. While not for everyone, the *Fantasy Coupons*, provide an opportunity to daydream about a non-committal encounter with no strings attached. For those who actually DO use them, good luck! You're gonna need it!

Let your imagination wander and enjoy our sidesplitting solutions to help us live together a little longer and a little happier!

For Males Only

Bored with jacking off to internet porn or girlie magazines? Want to stay true to your current lady but need a little variety? Join the Playmate of the Month Club!

PLAYMATE OF THE MONTH CLUB

For the low price of only $49.95 month, a new "playmate" is discreetly delivered to your doorstep providing you the variety that you seek with no negative side effects.

Pleasurable. Non-committal. No condom. Disease-free.

Made of non-toxic post consumer recycled plastic. Choose *Babe of the Month* and be surprised or pre-order ethnicity, size, shape and hair color to match your taste preference. Deluxe models available with a variety of options including the Screamer or the Glow in the Dark features. *No harmful effects have been reported by the overuse of this product.*

For Females Only

Is your guy's idea of a romantic evening a pizza and Saturday night sports on TV? Do you wish he was more attentive? Put the cuddle back in your huddle with Love Potion Number 9!

LOVE POTION NUMBER 9

Formulated with the all-natural hormone, OXYTOCIN, *Love Potion Number Nine* will spice up your life and bring romance back to your relationship! This elixir of love increases the desire to bond and form long term attachments. Available in handheld spray mist for only $19.95. The deluxe, convenient plug-in dispenser with remote control is available for the low price of $39.95. Regular use may result in the perfect man (or a guy who acts more like your girlfriend).

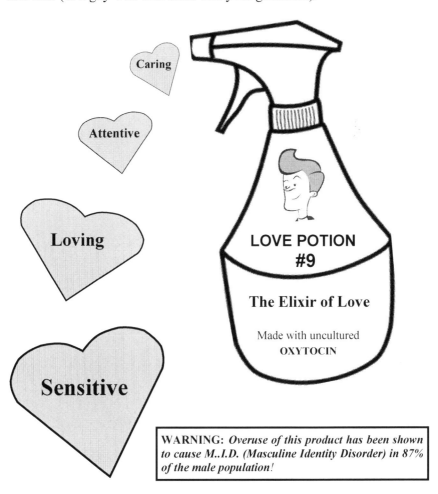

Caring

Attentive

Loving

Sensitive

LOVE POTION
#9

The Elixir of Love

Made with uncultured
OXYTOCIN

WARNING: *Overuse of this product has been shown to cause M..I.D. (Masculine Identity Disorder) in 87% of the male population!*

MALE FANTASY COUPONS

The Male Fantasy Encounter Coupon entitles the bearer to one night with a professional woman or that girl at the office you have been flirting with. Offers must be signed by both partners to be valid and each coupon is good for one cheating-encounter only. *WARNING: Use of these coupons carries **high risk** of fantasy dependency or divorce court! Additional coupons available upon request.*

Male Fantasy Coupon

A
Free Relationship Pass
Terms Must Be Agreed Upon by Both Partners
Offer must be signed to be valid.
Good for one visit only

Signature_____Date_____
Signature_____Date_____

Male Fantasy Coupon

A
Free Relationship Pass
Terms Must Be Agreed Upon by Both Partners
Offer must be signed to be valid.
Good for one visit only

Signature_____Date_____
Signature_____Date_____

Male Fantasy Coupon

A Free Relationship Pass
Terms Must Be Agreed Upon by Both Partners
Offer must be signed to be valid.
Good for one visit only

Signature_____Date_____
Signature_____Date_____

Male Fantasy Coupon

A
Free Relationship Pass
Terms Must Be Agreed Upon by Both Partners
Offer must be signed to be valid.
Good for one visit only

Signature_____Date_____
Signature_____Date_____

Male Fantasy Coupon

A
Free Relationship Pass
Terms Must Be Agreed Upon by Both Partners
Offer must be signed to be valid.
Good for one visit only

Signature_____Date_____
Signature_____Date_____

Male Fantasy Coupon

A Free
Relationship Pass
Terms Must Be Agreed Upon by Both Partners
Offer must be signed to be valid.
Good for one visit only

Signature_____Date_____
Signature_____Date_____

FEMALE FANTASY COUPON

For the woman who fantasizes about sex with someone new, including lots of romance to go along with it, here is a Female Fantasy Coupon. Designed for the lady who is extremely secure in her relationship as well as the girl who may be on the brink of breaking up—here's your chance to make your fantasy a reality! *WARNING: Use of this coupon carries **serious risk** of attachment to the "one-night stand" or a visit to the lawyer.*

Additional coupons available upon request.

Female Fantasy Coupon

A Free Relationship Pass

Terms Must Be Agreed Upon By Both Partners

Offer must be signed to be valid.

Good for one visit only.

Signature_____Date_____

Signature_____Date_____

Additional coupons available at: www.cantkeepmyspouseblissful.com

A Final Thought

Ernst Mayr, considered the father of modern biology, believed that human intelligence was a lethal mutation.

This book is a humorous but honest look at relationships between men and women and how the forces of evolution, biology, and culture have shaped our behavior.

In early human development, our drive for SEX was primeval, our need for SECURITY critical to our survival, but SENSITIVITY? As humanity moved forward in time, as did its intelligence, increasing sensitivity, not sex and security, may have set in motion the bitch and asshole revolution.

Higher intelligence gave rise to *self-awareness* and our greatest single liability—*arrogance*. It's what really separates us from the animals. It's why we lie, cheat and have wars. With increasing arrogance came vanity and a sense of entitlement. While the battle between the sexes for intimacy, fidelity, control, and power continues, so does the tug between our intellect and basic animal instincts.

In the end, you can blame males for being power hungry and treating women like crap but you can't blame men for having a sex drive that would kill a goat. Conversely, you can accuse women for using sex to tease and manipulate men, but not for being sensitive, nurturing creatures.

In truth, SENSITIVITY is why we are assholes and bitches,

having either to much or to little.

If Ernst Mayr was right, then we are all just basically

Early Humans

Modern Humans

References

Books:

Baker, H. D. R. 1979. Chinese family and kinship. Columbia University Press. New York.

Baker, R. 1996. Sperm wars: the science of sex. Diane Books Publishing Company. New York.

Barash, D. P. and J. E. Lipton. 2002. The myth of monogamy: fidelity and infidelity in animals and people. 227pp. Holt Paperbacks. New York.

Burr, Chandler (2003). The emperor of scent: a story of perfume, obsession, and the last mystery of the senses. New York: Random House

Cheney, V. 2004. The Sex Offenses and their Treatments: The Problem--The Solution--Commentary. AuthorHouse. Bloomberg, Indiana.

Coontz, S. 2005. Marriage, a history: how love conquered marriage. Viking Press. New York.

Dening, S. 1996. The mythology of sex: Chapter 3. Macmillan. New York.

Fisher, H. E. 1982. The sex contract: the evolution of human behavior. Quill Publishing, a division of Willam Morrow & Company. New York.

Fisher, H. E. 1992. A natural history of mating, marriage and why we stray: anatomy of love. 431 pp. Fawcett Books. New York.

Flam, Faye. 2008. The Score: How The Quest For Sex Has Shaped The Modern Man.

Freedom, M. 1970. Family and kinship in Chinese Society. Stanford University Press. Stanford, California.

Maines, R. P. 1999. The technology of orgasm: hysteria, the vibrator and women's sexual satisfaction. Johns Hopkins University Press: Baltimore.

Morris, D. 1967. The naked ape: a zoologists study of the human animal. MacGraw-Hill. New York.

Probert, R. 2009. Marriage law and practice in the long eighteenth century: a reassessment. Cambridge University Press. Cambridge.

Saunders, K. W. 2011. What the history of obscenity tells us about hate speech. NYU Press. 255 pp.

Journal Articles:

Baker, R. R. and M. A. Bellis. 1993. Human sperm competition: ejaculate adjustment by males and the function of masturbation. Animal Behavior 46(5):861-886.

Burgess, S. 1999. Hey baby, and other lies (one man's opinion about dating). Chatelaine.

Crawfurd, R. 1916. Of superstitions concerning menstruation. Proceedings of the Royal Society of Medicine. Vol. 9 (Sect Hist Med): 49–66.

Darby, R. 2003. Medical history and medical practice: persistent myths about the foreskin. Medical Journal of Australia 178(4): 178–9.

Hadhazy, A. 2012. Do pheromones play a role in our sex lives? Scientific American. Feb. 12, 2012.

Mayhew, T. M., L Gillam, R McDonald and F J P Ebling. 2007. Human 2D (index) and 4D (ring) digit lengths: their variation and relationships during the menstrual cycle. Journal of Anatomy 211(5): 630–638

Nocerino, E., M. Amato, A. A. Izzo. 2000. The aphrodisiac and adaptogenic properties of ginseng. Fitoteropia. 71:S1-5.

Numbers, Ronald L. 2003. Sex, Science, and Salvation: The Sexual Advice of Ellen G. White and John Harvey Kellogg in Right Living: An Anglo-American Tradition of Self-Help Medicine and Hygiene ed. Charles Rosenberg, 2003., pp. 218-220.

Paige K.E. 1978. The ritual of circumcision. Human Nature 40:8.

Patton, Michael S. June 1985. Masturbation from Judaism to Victorianism. Journal of Religion and Health.

Shelton, M. 2013. Masturbation kills: the dramatic history of self-pleasuring masturbation. Psychology Today July 4, 2013

Silberstein J., J. Grabowski, C. Lakin, & I. Goldstein. 2008. Penile constriction devices: case report, review of the literature, and recommendations for extrication. The Journal of Sexual Medicine 5 (7): 1747–57.

Nahid F. Toubia, Eiman Hussein Sharief. 2003. Female genital mutilation: have we made progress? International Journal of Gynecology & Obstetrics 82(3):251–261.

Zitman, M. 2006. Testosterone and the brain. Aging Male. Vol. 9(4):195-9.

Video:
TED Talks:
Bondar, Carin. 2013. The birds and the bees are just the beginning. http://www.ted.com/talks/ carin_bondar_the_birds_and_the_bees_are_just_the_beginning? language=en Last viewed on November 24, 2014.

Fisher, H. E. 2006. Why we love, why we cheat. http://www.ted.com/talks/ helen_fisher_tells_us_why_we_love_cheat?language=en Last viewed on Sept. 2014.

Fisher, H. E. 2008. The brain in love. http://www.ted.com/talks/ helen_fisher_studies_the_brain_in_love?language=en Last viewed on Oct. 2014 Last viewed on November 13, 2014.

YouTube:
https://www.youtube.com/watch?v=b6LNzCEgaxM

Websites:

Handfasting:
http://futurechurch.org/brief-history-of-celibacy-in-catholic-church Last viewed November 27, 2014.

Oxytocin:
http://www.psychologytoday.com/basics/oxytocin

Ambergris
http://www.ambergris.co.nz/   http://en.wikipedia.org/wiki/Ambergris

2D:4D Finger Ratios:
McAlaster, T. 2009. http://www.theglobeandmail.com/life/longer-ring-finger-bigger-profits/article1146622/

http://healthland.time.com/2011/07/06/penis-size-it-may-be-written-in-the-length-of-his-fingers/

http://en.wikipedia.org/wiki/Digit_ratio

Human Musk
http://www.scientificamerican.com/article/pheromones-sex-lives/

Aphrodisiacs
http://www.unexplainable.net/info-theories/
interesting_facts_worldwide_aphrodisiacs.php

http://www.unexplainable.net/info-theories/
interesting_facts_worldwide_aphrodisiacs.php

Masturbation
http://marriage.about.com/cs/masturbation/f/masturbatfaq2.htm

Thomson, J. R. 2014. http://www.huffingtonpost.com/2014/08/08/graham-cracker-history-sexual-urges_n_5629961.html Last viewed on November 23, 2014.

http://www.dominicantoday.com/dr/this-and-that/2006/5/2/12982/Cave-paintings-show-aspects-of-sex-beyond-the-reproductive

Judie Jewel is a retired educator, not a psychologist, anthropologist, nor marriage counselor. Her credentials in the relationship world come, instead, from the school of hard knocks with two divorces and three marriages under her belt.

Growing up as an only child, she developed a keen interest in literature. Books became a constant companion and as she grew, her love for print did too. But she would not write her first book until she was in her late 50's—*All Men Are Assholes, All Women Are Bitches.*

Judie is the wife of co-author, Dan Dourson, proud mother of three children, Austin, Tyler, and Angie as well as grandmother of four. She divides her time between the USA and Central America with Dan.

Dan Dourson is a biologist, illustrator, and author of seven scientific books about biodiversity and biology. His passion for the natural world has taken he and his wife, Judie, to the rainforests of Belize, the Amazon and other Central and South American countries. His humor and insightfulness were the driving forces behind the book. *All Men Are Assholes, All Women Are Bitches* is his first humorous book. His marriage to Judie is his second.

Jacob Marlin is executive director and co-founder of the non-profit conservation organization, Belize Foundation for Research and Environmental Education (BFREE). A serious conservationist and herpetologist since his childhood, Jacob also has a lighthearted side as well. His dry wit and life experiences provided insight and material for this, his first collaborative book.. Jacob divides his time between Belize and Gainesville, Florida. He is a divorced father of three.

We invite you to follow us on Facebook at All Men Are Assholes.

The book is available online at Amazon.com

We would love to hear feedback from you! Please take a moment to go to Amazon.com and give us a review!

Manufactured by Amazon.ca
Bolton, ON

28645363R10048